MEDIEVAL CASTLES OF ENGLAND AND WALES

Bernard Lowry

Published in Great Britain in 2017 by
SHIRE PUBLICATIONS
Kemp House, Chawley Pk, Oxford OX2 9PH, UK

29 Earlsfort Terrace, Dublin 2, Ireland
1385 Broadway, 5th Fl, New York, NY 10018, USA

Email: shire@bloomsbury.com
www.shirebooks.co.uk

SHIRE is a trademark of Osprey Publishing, a division
of Bloomsbury Publishing Plc.

A CIP catalogue record for this book is available from
the British Library.

Shire Library no. 837. ISBN-13: 9781784422141

PDF eBook ISBN: 9781784422165

ePub ISBN: 9781784422158

Bernard Lowry has asserted his right under the
Copyright, Designs and Patents Act, 1988, to be
identified as the author of this book.

Typeset in Garamond and Gill Sans.

Printed and bound in India by Replika Press Pvt Ltd.

22 23 24 25 26   10 9 8 7 6 5 4 3

COVER IMAGE
Front cover: The imposing gatehouse of Carisbrooke
Castle (Alamy). Back cover: A detail of architectural
relief showing the arms of Reigate, including towers
and a portcullis (Wikicommons).

TITLE PAGE IMAGE
Controlling the Isle of Wight and also built within
a Roman fortress was William fitzOsbern's castle of
Carisbrooke with a tall motte composed of layers of
chalk rock surmounted by a polygonal tower.

CONTENTS PAGE IMAGE
Its rocky site precluding an effective outer bailey
Harlech relied for its strength on an immensely
powerful gatehouse.

ACKNOWLEDGEMENTS
Images are Acknowledged as follows:

Alamy, pages 10 (top), 2, 11 (bottom), 12 (bottom),
14, 16 (top), 22, 44, 59, 62; Getty, pages 4, 31
(bottom), 62, 65, 72; © Historic England, page 47.

The following images were obtained from Flickr
under commons licences: Andrew, page 33 (top); Bob
Crowther, page 17; Claire Cox, page 21 (bottom);
David Merrett, page 21 (top); dw_ross, page 23 (top);
Elliott Brown, page 12 (top); Erin Brierly, page 8
(bottom); Frank Hebbert, page 32; Gidzy, page 69
(top); Giborn_134, contents page and pages 18, 51,
70 (top); James Clarke, page 9; James West, page
66; Keith Roper, page 20 (top); Lee Penney, page
6 (top); Maggie Stephens, page 19 (bottom); Mark
Hoogenboom, page 19 (top); Martin V Morris, page
8 (top); Matt Buck, page 38 (top); Rept0n1x, page 33
(bottom); Steve Slater, page 71.

The following images were obtained from Wikimedia
under commons licences: Andrew Walker, page
7; Brobad, page 64; De Facto, pages 13, 42–43
and 57 (bottom); Hchc2009, page 70 (bottom);
jeffpmcdonald, page 49; Lieven Smits, page 46;
Llywelyn2000, page 36 (bottom); Luke McKernan,
page 69 (bottom); Michael Garlick, page 67 (bottom);
Nessy, page 6 (bottom); Nilfanion, page 55; Poliphilo,
page 27 (bottom); Rob Bendall, page 20 (bottom);
Tony Hisgett, Page 31 (top).

All other images are by the author.

Shire Publications is supporting the Woodland Trust, the UK's leading woodland conservation charity, by funding the dedication of trees.

CONTENTS

CASTLES OF CONQUEST

WHEN DUKE WILLIAM of Normandy and his invasion fleet, perhaps consisting of 7,000 men, a third of them knights, with their horses, equipment and supplies, landed at Pevensey Bay in Sussex on 28 September 1066 he found a land already richly provided with fortifications, even if many of these were archaic. By the bay was the late third-century AD Roman fort of Anderida, part of a line of similar fortifications along the country's south-eastern and eastern seaboard. A corner of the fort, cut off by a ditch and bank, provided the basis for a temporary camp for William. He then moved to Hastings where, again, a fortified camp secured his base (its precise nature remains unclear). This pattern would be repeated as the invasion force moved along the coast and inland, the Normans using ingenuity in making use of the walls of roman forts and cities, Anglo-Saxon *burhs* (part of a national system of defended towns), prehistoric hillforts and even neolithic mounds used as cores for Norman castle mounds. The defeat of King Harold the following month left the country leaderless and with its army destroyed. Thus began a process that would see England and South Wales covered in Norman castles both great and small.

William and his knights, who excelled in the art of war, were part of an expansionist Norman elite that had already colonised southern Italy and Sicily. England would undergo a revolution, tying it more closely to the European mainland. The followers of William, soon to be bound to him by grants of land, would hold the land by ruthless means, their power bases being in the castles they built, many inserted into existing *burhs* to control and tax the local population.

Subsequently, a number of William's first conquests passed into the control of trusted and powerful knights and bishops.

Opposite: Old Sarum, one of many ancient fortified sites utilised by the Normans: a ringwork has been raised in the centre of the prehistoric hillfort. A town and cathedral would later occupy the rest of the fort's summit.

William the
Conqueror's
White Tower
at the Tower
of London, so
called because
its surface was
once rendered
and limewashed.
A modern wooden
staircase replaces
the vanished
forebuilding.

William
fitzOsbern's
eleventh-century
great tower at
Chepstow; the
remains of the
additional storey
are of a later date.

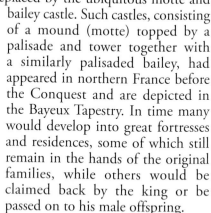

The means of securing a hold over the conquered country would be the castle: initially many of these would have been quickly erected circular earth and timber enclosures known as ringworks, often later replaced by the ubiquitous motte and bailey castle. Such castles, consisting of a mound (motte) topped by a palisade and tower together with a similarly palisaded bailey, had appeared in northern France before the Conquest and are depicted in the Bayeux Tapestry. In time many would develop into great fortresses and residences, some of which still remain in the hands of the original families, while others would be claimed back by the king or be passed on to his male offspring.

After securing his seaward bases at Pevensey, Hastings and Dover (at the latter using a prehistoric hillfort and Roman signal station site) and defeating Harold and his army, William moved inland towards London. Here he fortified a corner of the Roman city wall, later to be occupied by his great White Tower, and built two additional castles to secure his hold on the capital: Baynard's and Montfichet. From London he moved to Norwich (1067), then Exeter (1068) and he subsequently moved northwards to Warwick, Nottingham, Lincoln, Huntingdon and Cambridge. By the end of his reign in 1087, besides the county town castles, many smaller castles had been built to secure his hold over the rest of England and parts of Wales. During his reign great, strong towers and halls of stone were beginning to appear, influenced by French examples such as the great tower at Loches; at Chepstow, the White Tower, Richmond and Colchester (using the massive foundations of the Roman temple of Claudius, destroyed during the Boudican revolt of AD 60–61, and utilising the temple's surrounding wall as the basis for its bailey), as well as new masonry walled enclosures such as those at Ludlow and Richmond in Yorkshire where river ravines provided additional protection. In addition to these began to appear the motte and bailey castle.

These great stone towers and enclosures were atypical: most castles were of wood and earth resembling those portrayed in the Bayeux Tapestry. We have seen that the earliest 'new-build' campaign castles were probably ringworks: deep circular ditches with the spoil formed into banks topped by palisades. Within, accessed by a gate, would be simple living accommodation and stabling. Where topography

The massive great tower of Colchester, missing its uppermost storey, built on the foundations of a Roman temple and, with its chapel apse, resembling the plan of the White Tower.

The wooden church at Greensted in Essex, a remarkable survival from the time of the Conquest.

permitted it, a ditch and palisaded bank across a ridge could form the simplest of fortifications. The excavated Penmaen Castle Tower, Glamorganshire, is such an example: a small promontory ringwork by the sea with a gate tower and hall, of timber and drystone walling. Unlike masonry work, timber defences could be built rapidly and all year round (mortar could not be used in times of frost) and wood in lowland England and Wales was freely available. The disadvantages

Ludlow, built as a stone castle in the late eleventh century, its (blocked) gatehouse later converted into a great tower. An original hollow wall tower can be seen on the far left.

were that it was inflammable (the Bayeux Tapestry shows William's soldiers attacking the rebel castle at Dinan with fire) and was subject to rot. Despite this, the substitution of masonry for timber was slow: for example, the keep on the motte at the major castle of Shrewsbury remained a wooden one until the latter part of the thirteenth century.

The unique Greensted timber church in Essex, built at the time of the Conquest, gives an impression of how the timber walls of a Norman castle might have looked. To make the walls of the church tree trunks were split in half and trimmed to shape with an adze (a type of axe). All bark and perishable sapwood was removed. The original trees must have been of a considerable size. The half cylinders of heartwood were then set upright with their flat faces inward, morticed together to make a sturdy wall set in the ground.

In fact, the castles erected by William were not the first Norman castles to be built in England. A small number of Norman knights are believed to have built fortified residences in the 1050s, with the approval of King Edward the Confessor: Clavering in Essex, and three castles in Herefordshire – Richard's Castle, Ewyas Harold and Hereford – which were built along the troublesome Welsh border. What the original form of these pre-Conquest castles was is unclear, despite an archaeological excavation at Richard's Castle in the 1960s.

William's progress was not unopposed: the citizens of Exeter defied him in 1068, the city was besieged and on its surrender a castle with a stone gateway built in a corner of the city. In the same year York Castle was burnt after a local revolt. The castle and city was attacked again in 1069 and a second castle built, known as Baile Hill, on the opposite bank of the Ouse. In 1070 a Danish fleet, which had already attacked other Norman settlements in southern

The unusual, projecting, blocked Norman gatehouse of Exeter Castle: of interest are the two triangular-headed upper windows of Anglo-Saxon design, and, presumably, build.

To secure the troublesome south-west, strongholds were built including Exeter and the motte and bailey castles of Totnes, Trematon and Launceston (seen here), which was re-fortified in the thirteenth century by the Earl of Cornwall.

The simple, round-headed gateway to Shrewsbury Castle's inner bailey. In front is a small, primitive barbican formed of two musketry positions protecting the gate and dating from the English Civil War period.

and eastern England, attacked the city destroying the two castles. These were quickly rebuilt; it is likely that, as in the rest of the country, the workforce was the local pressganged and terrorised population, which led to even more resentment against the Norman occupiers.

By 1072 William had secured his northern frontier by defeating the Scottish king Malcolm, and shortly before this victory had despatched two trusted followers, Roger de Montgomery and William fitzOsbern, to secure the troublesome Welsh border, the first man becoming Earl of Shrewsbury and the latter Earl of Hereford. Both would establish powerful castles in their earldoms; at Shrewsbury the Domesday Book records the destruction of fifty-one houses during the castle's construction.

The conquest of southern Wales under the Normans would develop into a piecemeal land grab, with the castle as the means of retaining control. The Normans' principal base was at Cardiff where a motte was built about 1081 within the Roman fort, a mint also being established here. In the north of the

Cardiff's motte, its summit crowned by an octagonal shell tower, was built within the Roman fort. Additional work was carried out in the thirteenth and fourteenth centuries including the stone staircase and the forebuilding to the tower.

country a Welsh counter-offensive in 1105 brought about an uneasy halt to war, the Earl of Chester, Hugh d'Avranches, having met with only temporary success despite the building of motte and bailey castles.

William the Conqueror was succeeded on his death by his son, William II, also known as Rufus. His reign had hardly

The imposing great tower of Rochester, the circular corner angle turret marking the point where in 1215 King John's miners successfully brought down a portion of the tower.

The gateway through the massive ringwork at Castle Rising in Essex. The great tower is in the background.

begun when in 1088 there was a revolt by the powerful Bishop Odo and the siege of his forces at Pevensey. Odo retreated to the castle of Rochester, built in a corner of the Roman city, where he was besieged again, but starvation led to his surrender. Immediately after the siege a new castle of stone was built by Bishop Gundulph. William Rufus also built castles at Carlisle and at Brough in Westmoreland (the latter within a

The Roman fort at Portchester viewed from the great tower. The regular Roman walls and towers can be seen, together with the small enclosure of the Norman and later castle immediately below the tower.

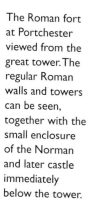

The great tower of Kenilworth, c. 1120, with its massive plinth and buttresses. The tower would see much alteration over the centuries, King John adding an additional stage with fishtailed arrow loops.

Roman fort) after he had seized the counties of Cumbria and Westmoreland from the Scots. This set the scene for future border wars, peace only being secured in 1237.

Following the accession of Henry I in 1100, a stone castle with a great tower was built within the Roman fort of Portchester, together with the construction of great towers at Rochester and Corfe and, probably contemporary with these, Kenilworth. At this time stone great towers were beginning to appear on mottes replacing those of wood, such as that at Windsor. The death of Henry in 1135 ushered in the Anarchy, a struggle for the throne between Henry I's nominee the Empress Matilda and the counter-claimant Stephen of Blois, Henry's nephew. War broke out, lasting twenty years, when, it was said, 'God and his angels slept.' The opposing forces built castles, some of which were built close to existing castles to act as siege works where forces could gather and access to the besieged be blocked. Examples of such castles, generally ringworks, can be seen close to the castles of Arundel, Corfe, Bridgnorth and Malmesbury. Matilda's son, the future Henry II, led an expedition from France to aid his mother, who was besieged at Wallingford Castle in 1153. The eventual peace saw Stephen remain in power until his death, with Matilda's son Henry succeeding him. One condition of the peace was that the unauthorised or 'adulterine' castles were to be demolished.

CASTLES OF SETTLEMENT

THE NORMAN VICTORY brought not only castles but the encouragement of settlers who could provide services for the local castle. The pattern of urban development is clearly seen at, for example, Devizes in Wiltshire and Richmond in Yorkshire, where the towns' growth follows the line of the curving castle baileys. These military boroughs, grouped around the security of the castle, led in turn to the development of planned walled towns such as Ludlow with their own charters. Eventually town and city walls would become increasingly sophisticated with mural towers and strong gateways.

The need for access to an important castle also led to the development of local roads (medieval kings were prodigious travellers: King John spent only one month of his entire reign without a move and this was in November 1215 when he was besieging Rochester Castle), helping markets flourish and services develop. From the town the local lord could obtain produce and labour and extract rents, taxes and tolls, fines and court fees. At other points along the Welsh border boroughs with castles were established to colonise the troublesome region. That the border environment was often uncongenial is evidenced by the number of failed boroughs, such as that at the pre-Conquest Richard's Castle in Herefordshire. Here, by the parish church with its detached tower, can still be traced the small, triangular marketplace. On the other hand, towns such as Chepstow, Hereford, Ludlow and Shrewsbury, protected by powerful lords and castles, prospered. Soon after the Conquest that other arm of the monarchy, the Church, began to establish churches, monasteries and other religious houses in the castle boroughs bringing further growth and prosperity.

Henry II was the first of the great Plantagenet dynasty, whose name originated from *planta genista*, the broom

Opposite: An aerial photograph showing the great tower of Dover Castle, its concentric walls, and the new work (below the great tower and inner bailey) following the French siege of 1216.

An aerial view of Richmond in Yorkshire showing the twelfth-century great tower built over the Norman gatehouse. Apparent is how the town, including the church and marketplace, nestle within the castle's protection.

Another town that developed around a castle was Ludlow in Shropshire, later provided with its own walls and gates. The connection of castle, town and church is apparent.

plant, a sprig of which was worn by the family as a badge. They were also known as Angevins, being descended from the counts of Anjou. For several centuries after the death of William I England would seldom be free from the fear of invasion. Henry and his wife Eleanor of Aquitaine also owned vast estates in France, and the peripatetic Henry would never

learn English. Much of his reign was spent fighting in France, Scotland, Wales and Ireland (the latter country would now see the introduction of the castle, Henry sending prefabricated timber castles to Ireland for the campaign). Henry tightened up the administrative and judicial systems of the country, regularising the Norman militia known as knight service of armed knights and their freeman followers, founded on the holding of land from the king.

Henry, half of whose revenue would be spent on castle building, built or modernised over ninety castles in his reign, which stretched from 1150 to 1189. It was he who began the great works at Dover, including the massive great tower, the work beginning in the 1160s under the direction of Maurice the Engineer. This work would be completed by Henry III. Castle building was the main form of royal expense, great works also being carried out at Newcastle, Nottingham, Orford, Windsor and Winchester.

English monarchs had to concern themselves with three frontier districts: the south coast facing France, and the Welsh and Scottish borders. In addition, the country's interior had to be controlled against internal revolt. The southern coast relied on the powerful castles at Dover, Arundel and Canterbury. In the north Henry II and King John spent large sums to secure the territory taken from the Scots after 1155: here the castles of Scarborough, Bowes, Newcastle and the episcopal castles

Monmouth's Monnow Bridge gate, although much altered, is a rare survival of bridge defences for a medieval town. A garderobe (latrine) projects over the river.

Defending a river crossing of the Tees in the north of England, Barnard Castle was one of a number of castles owned by Richard III.

(the Church was the largest builder after the king) of Durham and Norham, plus other non-royal castles such as Brough, Brougham, Middleham and Barnard, played their part. Along the Welsh border Henry spent less, relying upon the castles of the great Marcher lords whose string of castles ran from Chepstow up to the Earl of Chester's castles. Other powerful regional castles were those at Bristol, Gloucester, St Briavels (controlling the mines of the Forest of Dean as well as being a royal hunting lodge), Hereford, Worcester, Shrewsbury and Bridgnorth. Then there were the more exposed castles in the disputed areas, such as the smaller castles at New Radnor and Knighton in Powys. In addition, there were others such as the motte and bailey castles erected in the late eleventh century west of Offa's Dyke in the Vale of Montgomery. These appear to have been fortified farmsteads and, in a number of cases, working farms remain close to the earthworks.

In addition to the border 'hot spots' there would be continuous expenditure on the castles of the interior. Such castles as those at Kenilworth, Corfe and the Tower of London played an important part in the normal administration of the country, as mints and provincial treasuries, prisons, centres for tax collecting and local government and, in an age of constant royal progresses, as popular royal residences, such as Windsor Castle. On the borders castles would often change hands, be destroyed, then rebuilt, and then retaken.

Brougham Castle in Westmorland, built by King John to secure his lands taken from the Scots, straddled a strategic Roman road network. The early thirteenth-century great tower sits by the River Eamont.

Warfare turned upon the use of castles and was dominated by them. In a time of small-sized armies the castle acted as a force multiplier: a medieval chronicler described them as 'the bones of the kingdom'.

Henry II's most innovative work was at Orford in Suffolk, on a new site and begun in 1165. This had an unusual three-turreted great tower. The castle, designed both for military strength and comfort, was built to check the influence

The mass of Bamburgh Castle controlled a coastal road route into Scotland, and includes the great tower of Henry I.

Henry II's elaborate great tower at Orford, circular within and externally polygonal with three turrets.

of the powerful Earl Hugh Bigod whose castles in East Anglia, such as Framlingham and Bungay, were seen by Henry as a threat to his local authority. The shape of the tower was designed to overcome the dead ground at the base of the tower and the vulnerable corners of the square or rectangular great tower: however, these had not yet seen their day.

The volume of castle building in the hundred years following the Conquest meant that under the Plantagenets building work was largely a matter of developing existing sites. Even where there was the greatest of expenditure this was usually in connection with an existing fortress. Only exceptionally would an entirely new castle be built, such as Orford, and it was in a new area of conquest, Ireland, that there would be a volume of new castle building. The second half of the twelfth century saw a reduction in the number of non-royal castles being built as these became more under royal control. As siege warfare became more sophisticated the days of motte and

Conisborough Castle, built in the 1180s by Hamelin, half-brother of Henry II; like Orford, the aesthetic design was sophisticated. The small, early curtain wall towers are solid.

The simple twelfth-century great tower at Goodrich was carefully retained within the late thirteenth-century enclosure, whose corners are protected by elaborate spurred towers.

bailey building were over, unless for campaigns such as those in Ireland, and there was a steady replacement of timber by stone. But wooden defences remained as a convenient and easily repaired means of fortification: even at the new, royal Orford Castle the earliest outer defences were of wood. In 1204 King John is recorded as having financed the repair of the 'wooden castles of Shropshire', but by the end of the twelfth century there would be few royal castles not entirely of stone.

The great tower at Carlisle, subsequently reduced in height, is believed to have been built by the Scottish King Malcolm. The gatehouse is of the time of Henry II, the artillery work in the foreground of Henry VIII's time.

The simple great tower of Peveril Castle in Derbyshire. Romanticised in Sir Walter Scott's *Peveril of the Peak*, the castle controlled local lead mines.

The twelfth century onwards saw the appearance of comfortable royal apartments such as those at Richmond in Yorkshire and at Windsor where Henry II built or modified existing structures into royal apartments. Corfe Castle was a particular favourite of King John where much building was carried out including an external ornamental room, the Gloriette. Gardens are recorded at this time at Arundel and Marlborough. At Winchester there were dovecots and here King John ordered the construction of ovens large enough to roast up to three oxen in each at one time. Convoys brought wine to royal and lordly residences. Such attention to comfort did not detract from their military aspect, however, as the royal residence at Windsor successfully withstood a siege by the Dauphin of France in 1216.

The fashion for great towers developed further from the mid twelfth century onwards, even involving the modification and upwards extension of existing gatehouse passages as seen in the great towers at Ludlow and Richmond. New great towers were begun at Bamburgh, Carlisle (by the Scottish occupiers), Canterbury, Scarborough, Newcastle-upon-Tyne and Bridgnorth with other smaller, more basic towers such as that at Peveril in Derbyshire. Of these great towers, that built at Dover, facing France, with work beginning about 1180, was the last and most expensive to be built. Of Caen stone and Kentish ragstone, it had immense walls of over 20 feet in thickness, with a massive plinth, buttresses, a cross wall and a forebuilding with three flights of stairs containing a drawbridge, chapel, guardroom, and with piped water serving the keep. But at the time of its completion it was becoming obsolete as new designs of round or multangular tower were appearing in an attempt to avoid the dead ground and vulnerable corners of the square

The early, round-towered main gatehouse at Chepstow dating from the late twelfth century. The later Marten's Tower is to the left.

tower. Its builder, Maurice the Engineer, did, however, create the first concentric castle at Dover, with two lines of outer walls provided with square towers plus a twin-towered inner gateway. This mighty fortress would see constant development over the centuries.

A remarkable survival are the original doors from Chepstow's main gatehouse.

The advent of more sophisticated siege tactics led to the development of gateway defences, the castle gate being, generally, its weakest spot: in time this would lead to less prominence being given to the building of great towers, the developed twin-towered gatehouse often forming a great tower-like residence in its own right. An early example is the principal gatehouse at Chepstow, believed to have been built by William Marshal in 1189 and in the first year of Richard I's reign. Two strong round towers, fronted by a small barbican, with a portcullis, together with 'murder holes' and slots for dropping missiles or liquids into the gate passage plus arrow slits protect the gatehouse. Remarkably the original twin-leafed castle doors, recently dated by tree-ring analysis to the late twelfth century and therefore contemporary with the gateway, survive.

CASTLE DEVELOPMENT

AS WITH THE introduction of the motte and bailey castle in 1066, so approximately one hundred years later the next significant changes in castle design would come from France. The reign of the Plantagenets' French foe, Philip Augustus of France (1180–1223) saw revolutionary changes in castle design. The architectural confidence that inspired the great gothic cathedrals of France touched its castles, too. As with the reign of King John, Philip's reign coincided with war (against English possessions in France) and great castle building. Although the Romans had built fortifications in both countries with round towers, square towers had been the norm in the early middle ages. The *tour philipienne* of circular plan, with thick walls and stone-vaulted ceilings was more economical to build, was better able to resist fire if stone-vaulted, and gave greater protection against missile impact. It also overcame the principal weaknesses of the square tower: dead ground and corners vulnerable to mining. On the other hand, a square tower had better stability, its corners acting as

The earliest circular great tower is believed to be William Marshal's at Pembroke, built c. 1200, its upper floor vaulted. Around the summit of the tower can be seen the holes for the mounting of hourds.

stabilising feet, and its shape lent itself to more efficient room layouts; the more traditional square great tower therefore did not vanish in either country.

The earliest exponent of the great, round tower was William Marshal, Earl of Pembroke, who built the great tower at Pembroke. By building new castles in south Wales he hoped to contain the growing power of the Welsh prince, Llywelyn the Great. At Chepstow, as we have seen, he added a powerful twin-towered gatehouse, as well as similarly rounded towers along the curtain wall. Other great towers built in south Wales are those at Bronllys in Breconshire, and at Longtown and Skenfrith in Monmouthshire, all dating from the early thirteenth century. In time a variety of different patterns of tower would emerge such as the lobed tower represented by Clifford's Tower at York and Henry II's buttressed and turreted Orford.

A further compromise between round and square towers would emerge, represented by the round towers with square, spurred bases such as the late thirteenth-century Marten's Tower at Chepstow or the similarly dated towers at Goodrich Castle.

The great tower of Bronllys in Breconshire built on the motte of an earlier castle, one of several round towers built in the southern Welsh marches in the early thirteenth century. The builder, Walter de Clifford, was married to the daughter of the Welsh prince Llywelyn ap Iorwerth.

The accession of Richard I in 1189 did not usher in a spate of more castle building: in fact only six months of his ten-year reign was spent on English soil and his influence on castle building can be seen in France where he built the innovative Château Gaillard above the Seine in Normandy. After a long siege the castle fell to Philip Augustus of France. Richard himself would die during a siege, felled by a crossbow bolt during the siege of Châlus castle jn 1199. His successor John ruled during a period of great political turmoil, this fuelling work on ninety-five castles, including major works at Scarborough, Corfe, Kenilworth and Lancaster. On his sudden death in 1216 he was succeeded by the minor, Henry III.

Longtown in Herefordshire, built in the same period as Bronllys but of a more elaborate design with three projecting turrets (one containing a circular staircase). On the left side of the keep is a garderobe discharging onto the side of the motte.

The king's minority would last for eleven years, during which power was in the hands of William Marshal, Earl of Pembroke, the king's justiciar Hubert de Burgh, and the king's guardian Peter des Roches. The king had to rely on these three men together with castellans and sheriffs in order to resist a French invasion in 1216. When the French finally retreated repairs were required on the castles damaged by French siege engines. At one period the King was almost a virtual refugee in his own kingdom as the vital cities of Winchester and London were in the possession of the Dauphin Louis, who was making claim on the English throne. But Louis's hold was incomplete as some royal castles such as Windsor and Oxford remained in royal possession, while Dover and Lincoln were stoutly defended by loyal castellans. But it was becoming apparent that the country's castles were becoming obsolete in the face of modern siege warfare. On the departure of Louis Dover saw the introduction of new designs such as 'beaked' (pointed) towers, better able to resist missiles, and the castle's outer walls were extended to the cliff edge to complete the concentric layout introduced by Henry II. Other castles such as Rochester would also see their defences upgraded from 1220 onwards, this castle undergoing repairs outstanding since the damage caused by the siege in John's reign in 1215.

In 1234 Henry III came of age and took charge of his country and began to take an interest in his castles. Like other Plantagenets he was constantly on the move. Although much of his work has been absorbed by the work of later kings, we know that much was done as half of the country's revenue went on the king's works. The gradual replacement of timber by stone carried on, and royal castle building was now starting to surpass that of the king's barons.

In the second half of the thirteenth century France and England moved on divergent lines, with France continuing with the building of great towers while in England strength was increasingly seen to lie in powerful gatehouses and curtain walls and towers. The ingenuity of English master masons in building great towers now switched to the design of

Clifford's Tower, York, of c. 1240, replaced two earlier wooden towers on the Conqueror's motte: the first was destroyed in an anti-Jewish pogrom in 1190; its replacement was blown down in 1228. The plan is a quatrefoil with a now vanished central tower connected to the outer walls by a fighting platform.

elaborately defended gateways often protected by barbicans. This did not mean that great towers were totally forgotten, as seen, for example, at Edward I's Flint and in the elaborate tower constructed for Edward II's favourite Piers Gaveston at Knaresborough, or other fourteenth-century great towers such as those at Tutbury in Staffordshire, Pontefract and Sandal in Yorkshire.

The influence of the sieges conducted during the Crusades led to the need to make Western castles better able to resist siege attack. The ability to counter-attack from the newly introduced feature of postern gates (sally ports) led to a more offensive stance by the castle's garrison. The number of towers increased along curtain walls. The use of geometry in laying out a castle enabled these to be built in areas previously thought to be unsuitable, such as on flat land, with Flint, Rhuddlan, Harlech and Beaumaris adopting thoroughly geometric planforms. To resist increasingly powerful siege engines, ditches and moats

The powerful, spurred Marten's Tower at Chepstow. The tower was provided with its own portcullises, enabling it to be isolated from the rest of the castle. Note the carved figures on the battlements.

To provide archers with protection, merlons (the upright portion of the battlements) were provided with shutters against missiles. Here a reproduction shutter is set in a medieval bracket in St Mary's Abbey wall, York.

would widen, walls would become thicker as would towers, now round to better deflect missiles and with their bases battered to make mining difficult. Castle baileys became better planned to allow movement of the garrison and access to the towers and battlements, with merlons (the vertical section of a battlement) provided with shutters for the protection of archers.

In addition to archers on the walls, with the improvement in crossbow technology, arrow loops would be provided in towers and gateways, cleverly positioned so that a small number of archers could cover much of the surrounding ground. Some would have 'fishtailed' bases to give a wider splay and consequent better cover of the ground beyond the castle, while other loops contained horizontal slots (cross loops) for better lateral fire.

The point of entry to any castle is usually its weakest point. In front of the principal gateway might be positioned a small walled barbican (early examples are at Chepstow and Richmond in Yorkshire). The barbican at its most developed form can be seen at Goodrich in Herefordshire or at Conwy,

A suite of arrow loops with cross slots in the medieval upper portion of the Roman Multangular Tower, York.

both dating from the late thirteenth century, providing the first obstacle to the gateway and with its own drawbridge crossing the ditch. A further drawbridge connected the principal gate to the barbican. Above the entry might be one or more holes, known as murder holes, from which stones or boiling liquid could be poured onto an attacker who had reached the gate and who would also be under fire from crossbowmen.

Special attention was also paid to any bridge access across the castle moat or ditch. The Bayeux Tapestry shows wooden gangplank-like access to the motte top and such bridges could be easily destroyed in an emergency to deny access. A more satisfactory expedient used in later major castles was the use of a lifting drawbridge. This might be hinged or pivoted on its inner side with the bridge being drawn up by ropes or chains from a room within the gatehouse to rest against the external face of the gateway, this and the drawbridge pit adding a further obstacle to any attacker. A late medieval refinement, seen for example at Raglan castle, was a design of drawbridge which was suspended from counterbalanced horizontal beams, the upper parts lifting into wall chases on either side of the gate when the drawbridge was lifted, the lower parts into a pit.

In any major castle gatehouse was usually situated a portcullis, a vertically sliding grille of metal or metal shod to resist fire attack. In the developed castles of the late thirteenth

Castell Coch is a Victorian on-site reconstruction of a thirteenth-century castle. It gives a good impression of the suite of defences of a gatehouse: a drawbridge lifted by chains, a 'murder hole' in the vault and a portcullis: only arrow loops appear to be missing.

The late thirteenth-century gateway at Goodrich retains portcullis grooves, an arrow loop and 'murder holes' in the arch. Not visible is the adjacent draw-bar hole for the two-leafed door that withdrew – into the chapel!

century the use of portcullises would proliferate, protecting sally ports and internal entrances to larger towers such as Marten's Tower at Chepstow. The portcullis gave protection for the wooden twin-leaved doors of the entrance passage which, although closed by stout sliding wooden bars (draw-bars), were vulnerable to the battering ram. Although used by the Romans the portcullis first appeared in England from the late eleventh century, its use continuing up to the early sixteenth century. Its earliest appearance, arguably, was in the great tower at Colchester. Other early castles where a portcullis was used were in the great towers at Rochester and Hedingham in Essex. Widespread use of the feature started with the introduction of the twin-towered gatehouse. The portcullis was moved by a winch mounted in a chamber above the gate passage; such a winch can be seen at the Tower of London.

To further protect the base of towers or walls small square holes were placed running around the top of the tower or along the wall. From the beams inserted through the holes a wooden gallery could be erected, from which missiles could be dropped onto the enemy below. These were known as brattices or hourds. The remains of such holes can be seen around the top of Pembroke Castle's great tower. Although it was once believed that hourding was a temporary expedient it is possible that at certain castles, for example Flint, a permanent and decorative wooden gallery was built for both defensive and recreational purposes. The concept of temporary hourds was superseded by permanent stone galleries known as machicolation – as seen, for example, at Conwy's western barbican.

The latter part of the thirteenth century would see the country's greatest scheme of castle building: Edward I's castles in north Wales. But these would not be the only great castles built in Wales at that time. Lordly Caerphilly was begun in 1271 by Gilbert de Clare, who had virtual autonomy in

The extensive water defences of Gilbert de Clare's Caerphilly of the 1270s, built shortly before Edward I's return from the Crusades.

Bodiam Castle, built at the end of the fourteenth century by a knight engaged in the French wars, although provided with a moat, machicolations and circular gun embrasures, is more a defended manor house than a true castle.

Glamorganshire, and wanted to maintain his power in the light of the rise of the princes of Gwynedd and of Edward I. He had been present at the siege of Kenilworth in 1266 and it is likely that the water defences of this castle strongly influenced the design of Caerphilly. Like the slightly earlier Dover Castle, it was provided with powerful gatehouses, and was concentric. It had a great fortified dam to hold back the waters of its moats. Another great castle of the region was Kidwelly, extended in the early fourteenth century by the House of Lancaster and provided with a great keep-like gatehouse.

The thirteenth-century castle of Castell y Bere in Gwynedd controlled, from its rocky summit, a route from the west coast of Wales into Snowdonia. It was unusual among Welsh castles in having a sophisticated entrance provided with ditches and drawbridges, a barbican and flanked by a round and a rectangular tower.

The first Welsh war of 1277 saw Edward I attack Llywelyn ap Gruffudd, Prince of Gwynedd and ruler of three-quarters of Wales, who although having received royal recognition, was seen as a threat to the remaining Marcher territory. To consolidate their hold on their new territory the Welsh princes had themselves built stone castles. While not quite as advanced as English castles, they drew upon the advantages of the rugged Welsh landscape, the castles often sited in commanding positions, such as Dinas Brân ('Castle of the Crow') that towered above the key Dee valley route. The princes' castles also shared stylistic features such as the use of 'D'-shaped towers, such as that at Ewloe in Flintshire dating from the early thirteenth century. Carved stone recovered from, for example, Castell y Bere in Gwynnedd, indicate that the princes' castles were not lacking in style and comfort. English developments did not go unnoticed: the large round tower at Dolbadarn in Gwynnedd, equipped with a portcullis and garderobes (latrines), commanding a pass into Snowdonia, matches the vogue for round towers such as those of William Marshal in south Wales, while the twin-towered gateway at Criccieth, of the 1230s, may owe its origins to the Earl of Chester's castle at Beeston. Like a number of English castles, the Welsh castles often made use of earlier fortifications.

The survival of detailed royal building accounts enables us to examine in some detail Edward's mighty building campaign. His first step was to secure his southern flank and this was achieved by refortifying the motte and bailey castle at Builth by the River Wye; this had been destroyed by Llywelyn in 1260. To access the ruined castle, tracks had to be hacked through forests. Contemporary accounts show the employment of seven women at the castle who, with the rest of the workforce, worked every day, the only breaks being on church holy days.

The next castle of 1277 was a new foundation at Aberystwyth by the sea. In addition, a new town was established here. The work was financed by a loan from the king's banker Orlandino di Podio as well as by loans from the country's Jewish community. For the masonry work lime had to be despatched by sea from Tenby. Edward's master mason Master James of St George directed the work of other skilled craftsmen, with Master Giles of St George as clerk of works. Both men, plus other craftsmen, were from the kingdom of Savoy, an area in the western Alps now divided between Italy, France and Switzerland.

Dolwyddelan, also in Gwynedd, controlled, too, a route into the Welsh heartland. The rectangular keep seen here was restored in the nineteenth century.

A regular form in Welsh castles is the 'D'-shaped tower, as exemplified here by the one at Ewloe in Clwyd. Unusually, for a Welsh castle, it sits in a hollow: it is possible that it was more of a lordly residence than a true fighting castle.

Dolbadarn castle sits above the pass of Llanberis and was built in the thirteenth century, probably by Llywelyn ap Iorweth. The round tower's entrance has a portcullis. Comfortably equipped, it was to be the prison of the Welsh prince, Owain.

Another virgin site, also by the sea, was the castle of Flint where work began in June 1277. The castle and future town's name, coined at the time of its construction, may refer to the hardness or strength of the site. For this and future work in north Wales an immense assembly of men and materials from many counties of England converged on the port of Chester where the Cinque Ports fleet had been sent from its base on the south coast. Among the workers were diggers,

St Briavels Castle in the Forest of Dean controlled not only a vast hunting park but also the Forest's iron and coal mines, engaged in the manufacture of crossbow bolts on an industrial scale. The spurred and strong gateway now houses part of a youth hostel.

carpenters, woodmen, masons, smiths and charcoal burners (for the blacksmiths' forges). In August alone, 300 Fenland ditch diggers arrived escorted by three mounted sergeants to stop desertions. Timber was rafted by sea to the site. The accounts show that supervision was strict with deductions from wages for absenteeism or bad workmanship. A master plumber, William of Lichfield, completed the lead roof on the great tower, this apparently being an elaborate, perhaps arcaded wooden, structure.

By the fourteenth century the skills of England's carpenters had reached new heights with William Hurley's octagon at Ely cathedral being a prime example; Hurley also worked on the royal castles of Windsor and the Tower of London. The royal accounts also note the purchase of 'grease for the crane'. Such a crane might have been powered by a circular, man-operated treadmill. Bundles of straw were obtained to protect the works from frost over the winter.

To the west of Flint rose Rhuddlan Castle, close to an earlier motte and bailey castle of the time of the Earl of Chester's abortive campaign. To ensure sea access Edward had the River Clwyd canalised and this remains its current course. Master James was in charge again.

Despite the submission of the Welsh in 1277, in March 1282 Llywelyn attacked the still-unfinished castles of Aberystwyth, Flint and Rhuddlan. Lead destined for them was seized and used against the English by the Welsh in the attack on Rhuddlan, although the besiegers were beaten off by the king's cousin, Amadeus of Savoy. The accounts record the expenditure at this royal headquarters on work for the queen: a building for her goldsmith, a fishpond with seats, and a lawn with a fence made from wine cask staves. The castle hall was painted ready for the festivities of Christmas 1283. To the south another castle was being built at Ruthin.

The knight Sir John de Charleton, seen in this fourteenth-century window, was born in 1268 and was active on Edward I's behalf in Wales, building Powis Castle and acting as constable at the royal castles of Builth and Montgomery.

Edward I's castle at Flint was unusual in having a massive great tower detached from the inner bailey. Its height is now, sadly, much depleted.

The attacks by Llywelyn in March 1282 marked the beginning of the end of Welsh independence. Adopting a 'scorched earth' policy Llywelyn retreated into Snowdonia, destroying his castles. Edward was quick to repair and put them back into use, as well as building more new castles on an even grander and more massive scale, with workers and materials again travelling the length and breadth of the kingdom: from Northumberland to Sussex, Devon to Norfolk, all converging on the port of Chester.

The symmetrical, diamond-shaped inner bailey at Edward I's Rhuddlan with its opposing gateways.

Work began on the first new castle, Conwy, in March 1283, and it was completed in the remarkably short period of five

years, work being seasonal. This stands on a rocky ridge, which provided security as well as building stone, and there was an anchorage below. The king established his court here, and the queen was given a new lawn! New and powerful castles were also begun at Harlech in 1283, equipped on its rock with a powerful gateway, and in the same year Edward's masterpiece, the castle and walled town of Caernarfon. The latter was also the site of an earlier English castle and the reputed birthplace of Magnus Maximus, the father of the Emperor Constantine. However, a last, desperate revolt was mounted by the Welsh in 1294 when the unfinished Caernarfon was attacked.

The master mason for this mightiest of castles was Walter of Hereford and unusually it had polygonal towers and a banded decorative finish to its walls, possibly to resemble those of Constantinople, named after the Emperor. Its grandest tower is the Eagle Tower, named after a sculpture on a turret: it is believed that the tower was intended as the residence of King Edward's lieutenant in north Wales, Otto de Grandison.

A final link in the chain of Edwardian castles was the unfinished concentric castle of Beaumaris on Anglesey. For this castle men were again sent from Chester, the vanguard erecting a temporary camp. Again, this was under the direction of Master James of St George and Walter of Winchester was the clerk of works. Limestone for building work was burnt on site, for which 2,428 tons of sea coal was sent from Flint (Beaumaris had its own fortified harbour); for the wooden

The west barbican at Conwy. Having entered this constricted area an attacker would be subject to arrow fire from the two large corner towers plus missiles dropped from the stone bracketed machicolations above. The small towers were open backed.

Edward I's grandest castle at Caernarfon, with allusions to the city of Constantine, Constantinople, whose multangular towers and banded walls may have influenced the design of this most symbolic of castles. The massive Queen's Gate is far right.

constructions 105,000 nails were ordered. With the royal finances (somewhat unsurprisingly) in crisis and a new war with Scotland looming, the pace of work started to slacken and would never be completed.

In addition to Edward's castles there was lordly building at this time in North Wales: at Hawarden, Chirk and at the de Lacy Castle of Denbigh, begun in 1282. This had an ingenious gateway with three towers. The two principal gate towers faced the field while a third tower closed off the gate passage, the whole forming a vaulted courtyard. Provided with portcullises, gates and arrow slits the group of towers commanded the courtyard creating a killing zone.

The concentric walls of the unfinished Edwardian castle of Beaumaris on Anglesey, whose well-planned arrow loops comprehensively covered surrounding ground.

CASTLES OF CONFLICT

THE BASIC AND most prolific weapon of defence in the castle was the crossbow, although the shortbow could be used: the longbow made a gradual appearance from the late thirteenth century onwards. Although having a slow rate of fire the crossbow was powerful, had a flat trajectory and a range in the order of 200 yards; skilled crossbowmen were regarded as professional soldiers. The power of such weapons is attested by the twelfth-century chronicler Gerald of Wales who reported how an arrow pierced the oaken portal of a castle tower to a depth of 'four fingers'. Arrows and bolts for crossbows were ordered in vast quantities: for Edward I's campaign in Wales in 1277, 65,000 were ordered.

For longer-range firepower the trebuchet, mangonel and ballista were used for both offence and defence. The trebuchet was the largest siege weapon, consisting of a beam on one end of which was a sling for heavy stones. The stone was thrown by releasing the counterweighted opposite end, or by a number of men pulling violently with ropes on that end. One trebuchet, ordered to be built by Edward I, was his 'war wolf' whose construction required the work of fifty carpenters, and, disassembled, was transported by land and water to the siege of Stirling. The Scots surrendered but Edward still had to try out his engine against the castle walls.

The mangonel was a smaller weapon having a cup to hold the stone, projected by the torsion of twisted ropes or sinews. The ballista resembled a large crossbow mounted on a support: such weapons are believed to have been mounted at Criccieth and Harlech castles to give long-range protection to the small harbours below. Many of the leading English lords and even kings would have had experience of sophisticated siege operations carried out by both sides during the Crusades.

Although the number of documented sieges in England and Wales is relatively small, this does not mean that those described were the only ones. An early documented siege was that at Rochester in October of 1215. The accession of King John marked a period of anarchy with wars between John and his French-reinforced recalcitrant barons, with castles playing a crucial role. John's position was strong as he and his supporters possessed more than 150 castles.

Rochester Castle had been seized by rebel barons. Five royal siege engines battered the castle walls and an underground mine was built towards the southwest corner of the great tower. Once the foundations had been reached, masonry was removed and the wall propped up with wooden props. John gave the order to obtain 'forty fat bacon pigs, the least good for eating, to help fire the [inflammable] material we have gathered beneath the tower'. That the pigs did the job is apparent today, as the fallen square corner tower was replaced by a more up-to-date, slim, circular tower. Despite entry being gained to the great tower an internal partition wall protected the besieged until November, when hunger forced a surrender.

The following year, in May, a French invasion force landed in the south of England with the object of putting Philip

A trebuchet, its counterweight (right) drawn up for firing, has its sling (left) readied for release. A re-enactment in the grounds of Caerphilly Castle.

Augustus's son, the Dauphin Louis, on the English throne. Moving from Kent the invaders took London and then invested the great fortress of Dover, defended by Hubert de Burgh. The French had several siege engines including one named *Malvoisin* ('bad neighbour') together with 'belfries' (tall wooden towers covered in hides or metal plates) that could be pushed towards and overlook the walls. Although the outer walls of the castle were breached the French could not capture it. Other sieges conducted by the French were at the royal castles of Windsor, Berkhamsted and Lincoln. At Berkhamsted, which eventually surrendered, around the motte may still be seen the earthen platforms believed to have supported the French siege engines that rained down an incessant fire of missiles.

Using the assets contained in his loyal castles John mounted an offensive but died suddenly in October 1216. His successor was the nine-year-old Henry III. His accession, together with the issuing of a revised Magna Carta (John had largely ignored its provisions), revived the royalist cause. The siege of Dover was lifted in November 1216. In the following month Louis moved with his army and siege engines against the castle of Hertford, taken after a three-week siege. Louis then swung into East Anglia, seizing the castles of Hedingham, Pleshey and Henry II's modern castle at Orford; then Norwich and Cambridge fell. Prince Louis was left with a large swathe of the country from the Scottish border to the Thames, the only thorn in Louis' side being the castle of Lincoln; but in May 1217 William Marshal took the French forces at Lincoln in the rear. This defeat, together with a naval defeat at Sandwich in August made Louis' position untenable and following the Treaty of Kingston in September 1217 the French left England for good.

A further significant siege was that at Bedford in 1224 during Henry III's reign and after the first barons' war. Henry moved against the castle's occupier in order to restore it to its earlier owner and then decided to teach the rebels a lesson. Siege engines were brought from neighbouring counties and new ones built on site; 43,000 crossbow bolts were ordered and miners for digging ditches and cellars in rock were sent from the Forest of Dean. Stone was quarried for ammunition for the engines. A special tax was imposed on church estates to pay for the operation. Siege castles were built to observe the besieged and to prevent resupply. A constant bombardment was maintained. The outer bailey and then the inner bailey

were breached, while the miners tunnelled under the motte's tower. After holding out against the resources of the kingdom for eight weeks the castle surrendered. The majority of the garrison were hanged outside the castle walls; these were then dismantled and the ditches filled in.

The second barons' revolt, against Henry III in 1258, culminated in the longest siege on English soil. Following the death of Simon de Montfort at the battle of Evesham in 1265 his son sought to surrender Kenilworth Castle but his father's supporters refused this. The king brought to bear on this modern and strong castle a large army and a siege train. Stone-throwing engines were placed to the north, facing the great tower, while others fired across the mere, part of the castle's extensive water defences. However, the besieged also had stone-throwers, apparently superior to Henry's, and he was forced to send to the Tower of London for larger engines. The trebuchet could hurl stone balls weighing several hundred pounds for a distance of up to 350 yards and across the mere. During excavations in the 1960s some of the missiles were found in the outer bailey near a destroyed building. The castle's water defences denied the king the option of mining or moving belfries up to the walls and so a waterborne assault with boats was mounted but this failed. After holding out

for six months, disease and starvation forced a surrender – fortunately for the besieged on favourable terms.

In Edward I's Welsh wars his might was brought to bear against the small Welsh castle of Dolforwyn above a fording place of the Severn, and on the opposite bank of the river to the royal castle and walled town at Montgomery. The eruption of hostilities in 1277 gave Edward the opportunity of proceeding against Llywelyn's provocative castle. Siege engines were laboriously brought up to the castle's walls, one being transported by the Sheriff of Hereford's men from Wigmore Castle. Excavations have revealed missile damage to the castle's great tower although it was the shortage of water (many Welsh castles had no well but relied upon a rainwater cistern) that sealed its fate. No help arriving, the castle surrendered after a siege lasting just over a week. The badly damaged castle was repaired like other captured Welsh castles and put into royal service.

Another Edwardian siege was of Newcastle Emlyn Castle in 1288 when a siege engine was brought in sections on four carts towed by oxen and accompanied by cavalry and soldiers, with four hundred beach boulders being brought by packhorse for the engine from Cardigan, blacksmiths and woodcutters accompanying the siege train to make bridges and hurdles for the assault.

Drained of its water, the extent of Kenilworth's mere is now hard to reconstruct. To the left of the twelfth-century great tower are, firstly, the Earl of Essex's lavish Elizabethan apartments and, to the left of these, the medieval great hall.

BUILDING A CASTLE

T HE BAYEUX TAPESTRY (actually an embroidery as it is stitched, not woven) and knowledge gained from archaeological excavations are our main sources of information on early Norman castle building, which appears to have followed a pattern, either making use of ancient, existing fortified sites, such as the prehistoric fort of Old Sarum, or constructing on a 'green field' site. With the exception of a small number of high status masonry castles most of the Normans' early castles were of wood or, possibly, where stone was freely available, of drystone walling (the ringwork and bailey castle at Ashton Keynes in Wiltshire was of this construction, with a clay-lined ditch revetted with brushwood).

A major archaeological excavation was carried out in the 1960s at the 1070s motte and bailey site known as Hên Domen, close to its replacement, the thirteenth-century castle and walled town of Montgomery. Throughout its two-hundred-year history the castle remained of wood but was strongly constructed with many buildings in its bailey. Hundreds of horseshoe nails and some spindle whorls for spinning were found, indicating both military and domestic functions. Its construction was of massive upright timbers set in mortice-jointed sleepers. The foundations for a gangplank-like bridge, leading to the motte top, were found resembling those shown in the Bayeux Tapestry. The archaeologists also established that the castle was, from the outset, a motte and bailey castle and not a ringwork.

What might William's motte and bailey castles have looked like? The principal contemporary evidence is contained in the Bayeux Tapestry, a piece of propaganda to demonstrate William's right to the English throne. Created in England in about 1070 for exhibition in Bayeux Cathedral, it shows a

Now lacking its forebuilding, Castle Hedingham remains an elegant design. Of carefully cut Barnack stone, its uppermost windows were inserted for purely aesthetic purposes.

number of motte and bailey castles in Normandy plus the construction of a castle at Hastings. To build a modest-sized motte might take nine months. Time would be needed for the material – perhaps a sandwich of earth, stone, turf, earth – to consolidate before a wooden palisade and tower could be erected on its top. Baileys might be of an irregular shape but many mottes display a regularity indicating a laying out by the use of a length of rope and a peg to delineate the circumference.

At some earthwork castle locations only a motte is visible without a bailey. It is believed that the Tapestry images, although not representing an accurate image of a particular castle, give a valuable, general indication of the types of structure to be seen in the 1070s. They show, for example, the building of a motte said to be at Hastings with, possibly, a representation of the different layers of its construction. On top is a timber palisade but, as yet, no tower within. Other representations of castles in Normandy show wooden access ramps up to the motte top, elaborately carved, decorated gateways and motte top buildings, walls or banks surrounding the mottes and their attached baileys.

Within the gatewayed bailey would be the principal living accommodation: a hall, stables, a smithy, brewhouse, a chapel, kitchen, latrines and a water supply. Unfortunately, our knowledge gleaned from the few archaeological excavations

The great tower of Loches, central France, dating from c. 1020, is one of the ancestors of English great towers such as Rochester and Corfe.

of early castles is limited, although an excavation of the motte top of the small castle at Abinger in Surrey suggests that within the timber palisade running around the motte top existed a small tower built on wooden posts. A description by a mid twelfth-century chronicler gives a similar description for the tower on Durham's motte.

Like the Norman kings, the Plantagenets were always on the move and their presence was felt all over the land, especially in the construction of castles. At the time of that prodigious castle builder, Henry II, there was no office of works but there were master masons and skilled bands of workers moving on his orders. The king set major schemes, while the sheriffs dealt with the day-to-day affairs. At Dublin Castle, for example, King John's only involvement was in indicating where the keep should be placed leaving the sheriff to complete the job.

Berkhamsted, a classic moated motte and bailey site, controlled the northern route into London. To the left of the motte and on the far side of the moats are the tree-topped platforms for French siege engines dating from 1216.

With the accession of Henry III we hear the first mention of the office of Master of the King's Works, having overall authority over the skilled craftsmen employed on the works. Henry III was not a warrior king but had been born and bred in castles and appreciated their importance. He was once proud to arrange for a foreign visitor to be shown around the completed Dover Castle now with its concentric walls so that the visitor could appreciate the 'nobility' of the place. The king also expressed concern that the White Tower be kept white and that rainwater be channelled away from its coat of limewash.

The design and supervision of individual works was in the hands of the master mason. He was often referred to as an *ingeniator* (engineer) as he had other duties, for example looking after the king's siege engines or building bridges. Such men would have been acquainted with developments abroad – as, for example, the French-inspired 'beaked' towers of Henry III's Fitzwilliam Gate at Dover. He could draw upon other craftsmen such as master plumbers (who would construct leaden roof coverings), *fossatores* (constructors of moats and ditches), and master carpenters skilled in the construction of the elaborate roofs of medieval buildings. Some of the early *ingeniatores* were of sufficient importance to be named in official documents, such as Ailnoth, who in the 1160s was working at Windsor Castle and in 1173 on the Tower of London. Maurice the *ingeniator* is known to have worked for Henry II on his great keep at Dover. Such specialists were also put to use in demolishing castles as happened after the Earl of Norfolk's unsuccessful rebellion against Henry II.

Such men might also work on the great churches and palaces of the time: in the fourteenth century the great Henry Yevele worked on the fortified and cannon-armed west gate at Canterbury as well as working at Westminster Abbey and Westminster Hall. Where necessary foreign craftsmen were used, as they were for Edward I's castles in Wales.

The choice of a suitable castle site might be influenced by several factors. It might dominate an important communications point, such as a pass or river crossing, or be sited to control a centre of population. The local geology would influence whether a rocky site could be chosen or, in the case of the earliest castles, whether a ringwork or motte and bailey might be built. In areas of glacial drift deposits,

A medieval limekiln preserved at Carreg Cennen, a late thirteenth-century English castle in Wales. Its rocky site provided lime for mortar, render and the limewashing of its powerful walls and towers.

mottes might more easily be built, while in areas with thin soil, such as the plain of Glamorgan, ringworks seem to have been more common. The choice of the type of early earthwork castle was it seems, geology apart, no indicator of status and may have been a matter of purely personal preference. We have seen that the Normans often sought out pre-existing fortifications but they were not averse to using prehistoric burial mounds as the foundations for their mottes, as appears to be the case at Marlborough Castle.

Royal permission to build a castle was generally sought and royal licences to crenellate were granted. These might also be issued by certain powerful magnates such as the Bishop of Durham. Such grants conferred an official confirmation that an individual had been given permission to build a fortification, irrespective of whether it might be of doubtful strength, such as Stokesay Castle in Shropshire with its large hall windows and relatively thin walls, licensed in 1291. The extent to which such licences were issued is a little unclear as only a minority of castles appear to have been issued with such a permission, although this was, apparently, rarely refused.

Low-lying Whittington Castle in Shropshire relies largely on water for its defences. Originally a motte and bailey castle. its motte (left) was encased in stone and a relatively simple towered gateway (right) added in the early thirteenth century.

Bridgnorth
Castle's great
tower, destroyed
by gunpowder in
the English Civil
War. Here can be
seen the inverted
'V' form of the
lead covered
roof, possibly
also forming a
convenient water
catchment system.
From the castle
site can also be
seen a siege castle,
Panpudding Hill.

Once a licence to build had been obtained and the site had been chosen, for the more major castles architectural drawings would be prepared by the master mason, and a number of these survive for some great Continental churches. However, these were not working drawings as such but rather an indication of the design of the building which would then be marked out on the site. Geometry would be used to work out the 'footprint' of structures such as round towers by the mason using his large compasses, and, with his square, setting out the angles of the walls. The pegging out on the ground of two adjacent triangles would give a precisely square shape. However, medieval geometry was not foolproof and the slightest error led to distortions. Such is the case at Flint Castle where the inner bailey plan is not precisely square. On the other hand, four of Edward I's castles in Wales have been shown to use a common 40-foot diameter measure for their round towers.

How the craftsmen and workers appeared on site is shown in an illuminated thirteenth-century chronicle where a king is with his master mason; both wear gloves and long tunics, while the construction workmen wear short tunics but have no gloves despite the roughness of the stone. Masons are shown carving the stone with double-headed axes, while labourers operate a small crane to draw the finished stone up in a basket. Two 'setters' on the wall top are shown using a primitive but effective plumb level. Wooden ladders lead up to the wall head.

Many of the medieval building operations shown in this and other illustrations are similar to modern techniques but without the refinement of engine power. Scaffolding was also of wood, being secured in the rising walls by putlog holes to contain the wooden scaffold supports, their horizontal or helicoidal lines still visible today. On removal of the scaffolding the holes would be filled with render. Lime mortar was mixed in a large trough, lime often being burnt on site.

Building was a seasonal activity and probably tapered off when harvest labour was required, halting in the winter. To construct four to five feet of walling per season was considered good going. Some sites had plentiful stone for building;

Sitting on its hill above the flat Cheshire plain and occupying the site of a prehistoric hillfort, Ranulph of Chester's early thirteenth-century Beeston Castle's random masonry would once have been rendered and limewashed, its white form being visible for miles.

Montgomery Castle, its power eclipsed after the building of Edward I's great Welsh castles, guarded an important crossing point of the Severn. To the left is the Well Tower and to the right can be seen the early thirteenth-century solid-fronted gateway.

others had little. Where fine limestone was available a great tower such as that at Conisborough in Yorkshire might be faced in a smooth and gleaming, unrendered stone with a rubble stone core. The great tower of the twelfth-century Hedingham Castle in Essex, while using local flint for the core of the walls, required fine Barnack stone brought from Northamptonshire. The eleventh-century White Tower of London used Caen limestone shipped from Normandy, Kentish ragstone and Reigate Stone for finely dressed work such as doors or windows. At Beeston in Cheshire, also built on the site of a prehistoric hillfort, where stone was taken from the castle ditch (wedge holes for quarrying are still visible), a rougher appearance would be acceptable as, once covered in render and limewashed, the castle's walls would present a gleaming appearance. At Conwy, stone for most of the work was available on site with sandstone being shipped from Chester for the fine mouldings for doors and windows.

Despite the functionality of castles, great pride was taken in their appearance. It is possible that where roof tiles were used, these might have been glazed: green examples have been found at the moated site at Brockhampton in Herefordshire. Glazed floor tiles were also certainly used in the grander castles.

Where a major source of water was available a moat provided an effective barrier. Water might come from different sources: a river or brook, for example the Thames at the Tower of London or the watercourses feeding the mere at Kenilworth; the sea at Flint; or by natural springs such as those at Whittington Castle in Shropshire, which was also sited within the banks of a prehistoric fort. A moat inhibited tunnelling towards the castle as there existed the risk of the flooding of any excavation. Alternatively, a deep, dry ditch could be dug, although it was less effective as its depth could be determined and be filled with brushwood to enable an attacker to approach its walls.

The larger castles would also need a reliable source of domestic water. This was essential for cooking, brewing and cleaning as well as for extinguishing fires. At Rochester a well was constructed within the great tower and water was moved around the interior by pipes. At other great towers, the lead 'M'- or 'V'-shaped recessed roofs might act as a water catchment area for water storage or the flushing of garderobes. In the roof of Conisborough's great tower cisterns remain.

Considerable efforts were often made to access water: at Beeston the well in the inner bailey is over 300 feet deep and is for 200 feet masonry lined with a solid rock shaft below this. At Montgomery Castle, begun in 1233, twenty miners from the Forest of Dean sank a vertical shaft 210 feet from the castle rock to a point where, on rock below, vegetation indicated the presence of water. The Well Tower was built around the shaft. At Chepstow a stone shaft ran down the cliff to a spring by the Wye edge, water being drawn up by a bucket. Castles built by the Welsh princes, in a country of high rainfall, largely relied on cisterns although at least one well is known, at Caergwrle where, after the castle was captured by Edward I, a barrel of water was sent to him after the well had been cleaned.

In the late thirteenth century, castles reached new heights of sophistication. This hand basin was fed from Goodrich Castle's well.

LIFE IN A CASTLE

IN ITS DEVELOPED form the castle performed many functions: stronghold, store for weaponry, barracks, home, centre of government, justice and administration, prison and hunting lodge. The constable dealt with day-to-day affairs and controlled a small garrison. Local knights performed castle guard duty in exchange for their lands. An early fifteenth-century manuscript records the areas of responsibility at Richmond Castle in Yorkshire of eight local knights.

How one lived in the castle depended on one's status and that of the castle. For example, for the garrison of the small but important motte and bailey castle of Hên Domen in Montgomeryshire, established in the eleventh century by Roger de Montgomery to guard a ford across the Severn, archaeological evidence indicates a life of simplicity with cooking done in coarse wares and with only one coin (of King John) being recovered, indicating a largely self-sufficient existence with local bartering. On the other hand, for Henry III's stay at Marlborough Castle in 1236, 40 pounds of imported dates, boxes of figs and pressed grapes, packets of 'good ginger' and towels were sent for use at Christmas. In addition to a liking for herrings, Henry also had a fondness for salmon pasties. In addition, wine for the king coming from Anjou and Gascony was plentiful. His retainers would have been richly clothed and food and drink would be served on or in expensive imported pottery.

Religious observance required the eating of fish on Fridays or on certain holy days: fish could be obtained from rivers or the sea and there were often fishponds close to a castle. Meat was fresh or salted (the latter stored in castle basements with the wine). Venison came from the hunting parks. Pigeons were an important part of the medieval diet and dovecotes were common, Barnard Castle having a Dovecote Tower. Rabbits were another staple food, warrens being built outside castles and manors. For great religious feast days lordly feasting would be the norm: at Easter 1297 in Goodrich Castle, sides of beef and bacon, unsalted pork, half a boar, half a salmon (all these from the castle's stores) plus purchased beef, mutton, kid, capons and hens, two veal, six hundred eggs, pigeons and cheese (brought by boat) were made available.

Conwy had a water-powered mill by its side together with a wharf for bringing in food in a hostile environment. The kitchens, in addition to cooking meat, had ovens for roasting barley for brewing, and baking bread and pastries. Day-to-day meals, as at Caernarfon, consisted of meat boiled and the flesh removed for the second course, the first course being a pottage of the meat broth mixed with oatmeal and vegetables, eaten from wooden bowls or with flat loaves of bread providing a rudimentary platter. At Restormel Castle in Cornwall at Christmas 1362, Edward the Black Prince, Duke of Cornwall, who was visiting his castle, was accommodated in the privileged inner sanctum of the great tower. His party consisted of up to fifty people together with their horses and they brought furniture and tapestry hangings for the festivities. Wine was in the castle and the tower's kitchen served food via a servery partition, to minimise the risk of fire spreading from the ovens. The castle had a piped water supply via a conduit serving each 'house of office'. The nearby deer park, stocked with three hundred animals provided adequate hunting and meat for the kitchens.

We have seen that medieval kings took an interest and pride in their castles. This also applied to the castles of their subject lords. The great towers and halls were intended to awe a visitor by their scale and grandeur. At the de Vere castle of

The presence of a grand fireplace denoted status and this is a fine example from Conisborough's great tower. Note the 'joggled' lintel and finely worked stone.

Complementary to the fireplace in importance was the chimney. This fine example is from St Briavels Castle, topped by a hunting horn.

Hedingham in Essex the upper-floor windows were merely aesthetic, looking onto the roof gutters. Below this level existed two large heated and grand rooms; below this was a basement. Apparently there was no sleeping accommodation in the tower. The grandest was the third floor with a gallery looking down into what must have been an opulent room and out towards the countryside. On reaching a great tower one might be greeted by a richly carved doorway into the forebuilding, such as that at Castle Rising in Norfolk, from which rose a broad staircase leading to the first floor where the daily affairs of the castle and estate were conducted. The upper floor contained the lord's hall for his accommodation and that of his guests, if the accommodation buildings in the bailey were not being used for this purpose. Here would be the grandest windows, facing for safety into the castle's interior closed by wooden shutters (glazing would make an appearance from the thirteenth century) and with a large fireplace providing heat and light. At the great tower of Rochester smoke from the fireplaces on all floors exited through vents in the wall. Later medieval castles had elaborate fireplaces, such as those at Conisborough. Chimneys were also regarded as a mark of status and fine examples can be seen at St Briavels in Gloucestershire and Grosmont in Monmouthshire. Smaller great towers such that at Peveril in Derbyshire show no fireplaces and may have been heated by charcoal braziers.

Richly decorated walls and ceilings, tiled floors and wall hangings were designed to impress. In 1256 the fastidious Henry III employed a painter at the royal castle of Guildford to marble the hall's pillars and to spangle the great chamber's green ceiling in gold and silver. Edward I employed a Savoyard painter, Stephen, to adorn his new apartments in his Welsh castles with a then-fashionable red and white chevron pattern.

Church and state were close and many castles contained a decorated chapel provided with a small basin (piscina) for washing the sacred vessels and an aumbry for their storage. The window, usually facing east, might be the only one provided with glass, possibly stained. As well as ministering to the castle's souls, the incumbent priest might act as a scribe, accounts keeper and educator of the lord's children.

Fire was also used for cooking: this baking oven is from the great tower of Orford and has an arch of medieval roof tiles.

Lordly washing was done in large wooden tubs, most likely empty wine barrels, with warm water brought by servants. At Goodrich water piped from the castle well fed basins for hand washing. Considerable care was taken over the disposal of human waste to avoid disease and the contamination of the water supply. At its most basic level, at Hên Domen near Montgomery archaeologists found a covered latrine operating on a deep-litter basis containing waste charcoal, bracken and wood shavings to compost the excrement. The keep of the small masonry castle of Peveril in Derbyshire was provided

The forebuilding at the great tower of Castle Rising was designed to impress. Visitors entered through a large decorated door and proceeded by way of a staircase to the first-floor audience chamber.

Major castles had the services of a priest who, at Orford, had his own chamber. The small arcaded chapel, squeezed into one of the turrets, retains the altar and to the right is the piscina for washing the sacred vessels plus two cupboards (aumbries).

with a toilet, also known as a garderobe, discharging over the side of the keep onto the rocks below. Other major castles such as Rochester were provided with a cesspit that would be cleared periodically, while at other castles latrines would discharge into the moat.

Not all castle life was military grimness. The twelfth-century chronicler Gerald of Wales tells us that at his place of birth, the castle of Manorbier in Pembrokeshire, 'just beneath

Manorbier was the birthplace of the twelfth-century chronicler Gerald of Wales. Although the castle was remodelled after Gerald's time the façade is of interest as it shows the line of earlier battlements provided with arrow slits beneath a later heightening of the wall.

its noble walls is a very good fishpond, notable for its majestic appearance and depth of its water. On the same side there is likewise a most beautiful orchard, enclosed between the pond and a wooded grove – itself remarkable for both the rocky crags and tall hazel trees.'

Eleanor of Castile, the wife of Edward I, was an enthusiastic gardener, and she established gardens at the new castles of Rhuddlan and Conwy. In addition, at the latter castle and in the security of the east barbican, she planted a private garden. An account of the fourteenth century describes the presence of vines or trailing plants and a later account describes there being ornamental flowerbeds. At Clun a late thirteenth-century rectangular tower was built on the side of the motte to accommodate the FitzAlan family, Barons of Clun, and their guests, who might enjoy fishing in the castle's ponds or spending time in the 'pleasaunce', an ornamental pavilion set in a formal garden. At the castle of Owain Glyndŵr at Sycharth in North Wales, still a motte and bailey castle, the court poet Iolo Goch describes the motte as being 'encircled by a moat', and 'beyond, an orchard,

The extensive earthworks and outer works of Clun Castle in Shropshire incorporated formal gardens and fishponds. A late thirteenth-century great tower sits ostentatiously on the side of the motte.

The irregularly shaped great tower of Berkeley in Gloucestershire, enclosing an earlier motte, was the prison and setting for the brutal murder of Edward II.

vineyard, rabbit warren, mill, dovecot, fishpond with pike and salmon, and a deer park'. Peacocks and herons are also mentioned in the account.

At the late medieval castle of Raglan orchards full of apple trees, French plums and pears, figs, cherries, grapes, nut trees and 'every fruit that is sweet, and delicious' are described. At Tretower Court and Castle a mid-fifteenth-century garden has been recreated with an arbour and pavilion, vines, roses and honeysuckle. The gardens are enclosed with trellising, with fountains, chequerboard flowerbeds; turf seats; herbs; irises and lilies are grown: and

The principal state prison was the Tower of London, in use until modern times. This postcard, dating from just after the Second World War shows (left) Traitors' Gate, built in the thirteenth century as a royal water gate. To the extreme right is a 1940 pillbox covering the riverfront of this still-important site.

THE TOWER OF LONDON AND RIVER THAMES

all apparently well-attested elements in western European gardens of the later Middle Ages. We can also imagine at many castles herbs being grown to sweeten the air of castle rooms or for use in the kitchen.

With walls strong enough to keep the unwanted out, such walls could be used to detain prisoners. Ironically, at a number of castles it would be the king himself who might be a prisoner and some would perish therein. Edward II met an unpleasant end in Berkeley Castle, Richard II died in Pontefract Castle, and Henry VI perished in the Tower of London. The latter continued as a place of confinement into the early 1950s and the execution of the last German spy on British soil in the Second World War, Josef Jakobs, was carried out in 1941. In this war the Tower also constituted one of three places in London nominated as 'keeps' of last resort where, if London was invaded, the strongpoints would be held to the last man and last bullet. More fortunate was John II of France, a prisoner of Edward III, who was held in comfortable confinement in a number of royal castles before his release following the payment of a huge ransom (which provided funds for Edward's lavish work on Windsor Castle) in 1360.

For the common man, imprisonment was, generally, a temporary matter while awaiting the king's justice. Prisoners were often accommodated in gate towers under the control of the gatekeeper, and the underground tower 'dungeons', beloved of gothic novelists, were more likely to be used for the storage of wine or salted meat. However, a small underground room with external sliding bolts at Goodrich Castle may have been used for the imprisonment of poachers and other malefactors. That imprisonment was not always very secure is evidenced by a petition to the king by the keeper of prisoners in Guildford Castle outlining that it was too weak to keep captives, leading to the escape of fourteen prisoners in 1391.

Believed to have been built as a prison (it is locked from the outside), this unlit and unheated underground room is at Goodrich Castle.

LATER YEARS AND DECLINE

FROM THE ELEVENTH to the end of the thirteenth century English kings had been the leading founders and maintainers of castles as the means for the execution of royal policy in England and Wales. The symbolic place of birth of Edward I's son, Edward II, at Caernarfon Castle in 1284, later to be created Prince of Wales and Earl of Chester, began a process by which the responsibility for some of the more important of the king's castles was passed to royal sons. In 1337 the Duchy of Cornwall was created by Edward III to be automatically passed to the monarch's eldest son. In 1399 the Duchy of Lancaster, although established in 1267 for a royal son, transferred responsibility for a number of important royal castles. The Prince of Wales assumed responsibility for the great Edwardian castles plus a number of the important castles in south Wales. The first Prince was assisted by an office based in Chester controlled by one of his father's foremost master masons, Master Richard the Engineer who had also been responsible for the king's trebuchets at Caernarfon Castle. He would become a prominent local figure, becoming Mayor of Chester and being given gifts, for example a mill and a farm. General supervision fell to a master carpenter: other expertise would be largely brought in on an *ad hoc* basis, as would be the case in the other two duchies. Craftsmen might be exchanged: for example, two masons came from the Duchy of Lancaster's castle at Pontefract to advise on the building of a new tower at Tutbury (later to be a place of imprisonment for Mary, Queen of Scots) in 1441; the great tower had enjoyed a renaissance in the late Middle Ages.

Edward III, whose reign began in 1330, is principally known for his new work at Windsor Castle, financed by his wars with France and especially the French ransom paid

Opposite: Edward III carried out extensive works in the upper ward at Windsor, including the enlarging of the great tower on the motte. Henry VII's St George's Chapel can be seen in the lower ward.

for the return of the captured French King John II in 1360. The work involved such magnificent non-military projects such as the chapel of St George (the beginning of a cult of the saint), although work was also carried out on the great tower on the motte together with a new gatehouse and grand lodgings, many of the new ancillary buildings being of timber including those within the great tower. It is not surprising that Edward preferred to stay at Windsor Castle, with its new and magnificent buildings and great hunting park than at the king's palace of Westminster.

The fourteenth century is said to have been the greatest building period of the middle ages. If royal castle building declined, this did not mean that new lordly castle building or work on existing castles slackened. Lordly wealth required comfort with ostentation. Important examples are the splendid works at Warwick Castle between 1360 and 1390 by the earls of Warwick, and at nearby Kenilworth, where work transforming the water-bound castle into a comfortable and palatial residence carried on into the age of Elizabeth I. At Warwick, apart from a strong gatehouse, new towers were

The introduction of brick in the later Middle Ages encouraged the decoration of walls, as seen here at the uncompleted Kirby Muxloe of the 1480s, its walls and square towers provided with gun embrasures.

built overlooking the Avon: the tri-lobed Caesar's Tower showing French influence (Thomas, Earl of Warwick, had fought in the French wars) and the twelve-sided Guy's Tower.

Elsewhere in the Midlands the symmetrical moated Maxstoke was built in the 1330s and in the following century the similarly symmetrical brick-built Kirby Muxloe, which was provided with gun embrasures. This castle was never finished: its creator, Lord Hastings, was a victim of the political upheavals of the late fifteenth century and fell foul of Richard III, suffering summary execution. Kirby Muxloe was one of a number of late medieval castles, built principally in the eastern and southern counties, where the newly fashionable brick was used. The use of different coloured bricks enabled the decoration of walls and the new castles often exhibited elaborate gateways; prominent examples are the castles of Herstmonceux in Sussex, Caister in Norfolk and the surviving great tower at Tattershall in Lincolnshire.

At the beginning of the fourteenth century Thomas, Earl of Lancaster, built Dunstanburgh Castle on the coast of Northumbria, but suffered a similar fate to the builder of

Among the mightiest towers of the later Middle Ages, obviously designed to impress, are the fourteenth-century Caesar's Tower (right) and Guy's Tower (upper centre) at Warwick, flanking a very strong gatehouse. To the left is a landscaped motte.

Situated remotely on the Northumbrian coast, the early fourteenth-century Dunstanburgh Castle, with its great gatehouse, did not prevent its powerful owner, Thomas of Lancaster, being captured on the orders of Edward II and executed in 1322.

Kirby Muxloe. Also in the north a strong, angular gatehouse was built at Lancaster Castle in the early 1400s and, slightly before this, Richard le Scrope, Treasurer of England, built the four-square Bolton Castle in Yorkshire, provided with a number of self-contained suites. Two Yorkshire castles, Sandal and Pontefract, saw ongoing and important work during the fourteenth century and into the fifteenth, under both royal and lordly ownership.

Other important works by powerful local magnates are exemplified by the work of the Percy family at Alnwick and Warkworth in Northumberland. In this often lawless border region we should also mention the small towers, known as 'bastle' or 'pele' houses, built by the less well-off landowners as a protection for themselves, their families and cattle in times of danger. It follows that similar structures were built on the other side of the restless Scottish border.

While royal and lordly castles were being made grander and more comfortable (without necessarily compromising their strength) the rising middle classes in lowland England were building, from the late thirteenth century onwards, increasingly commodious but lightly fortified houses for themselves and their families. One of the earliest is Stokesay Castle (*c.* 1270) in Shropshire, which, while having a moat and thin stone towers, had its large and vulnerable hall windows facing outwards. Other examples are the moated houses of Ightham Mote in Kent and Baddesley Clinton in Warwickshire. At the latter site a drawbridge and gun ports were provided in the gatehouse. Such houses were often bypassed in the English Civil War and remain as picturesque reminders of these smaller fortified sites.

In the fourteenth century the face of warfare was slowly changing with the introduction of gunpowder. The increasing power of artillery would eventually drive significant changes in the design of fortifications over future centuries but these would not occur until the advent of the Tudors. The first guns in castles were largely small anti-personnel weapons.

Using Roman stone and close to Hadrian's Wall, the Vicar's Pele at Corbridge in Northumberland was a place of safety for a cleric in the fourteenth century on this troublesome border.

Nunney Castle in Somerset, dating from the late fourteenth century, displays a French influence: its builder, Sir John de la Mare, had fought in France.

The late thirteenth-century castle of Stokesay in Shropshire: its large hall windows, closed internally by wooden shutters, belies its castle status. Of interest is the original wooden, jettied domestic gallery to the left giving a flavour of the appearance of defensive hourds.

In siege warfare the mangonel and trebuchet remained no less effective than the early cannons known as bombards. The earliest gun-armed fortifications were built on the south coast during the wars with France in the fourteenth century: at Cooling in Kent and at Bodiam in Sussex. Despite their up-to-date armament, neither castle could be considered strong: the moat at Bodiam, for example, could have been quickly drained by a small party of men, and its gun embrasures are inconveniently sited. The existing west gate at Canterbury and the gatehouse at Carisbrooke Castle on the Isle of Wight were enlarged to receive gun embrasures in the 1380s.

In addition to wars with France and Scotland the late Middle Ages would see a final Welsh war when, in 1400 Owain Glyndŵr declared himself 'Prince of Wales'. Improvements to Kidwelly Castle, principally a powerful new gatehouse, had begun in the wake of the rising power of Glyndŵr, to be completed just in time by Henry IV. By 1403 he had occupied much of Wales, raiding towns held by English and besieging their castles: even the great Edwardian castles of Aberystwyth and Harlech surrendered to Owain in 1404. Harlech would hold out until 1409 when it succumbed to English bombards.

The popularity of great gatehouses continued into the beginning of the fifteenth century. This is Henry IV's great castle gatehouse at Lancaster.

The popular song 'Men of Harlech' refers to a later siege in 1468 during the Wars of the Roses when, incidentally, the royal siege train's bombards forced the surrender of the castles of Alnwick and Dunstanburgh in Northumbria. Directing the siege of Harlech for the Yorkist side was the immensely rich and powerful William Herbert, created Earl of Pembroke by

Cooling Castle in Kent is, like Bodiam, another somewhat weakly defended castle of the late fourteenth century built during a period of unrest with France. Like the latter castle it has circular gun embrasures and extensive machicolations.

The great gate at Kidwelly, built in a local style, and begun at the end of the fourteenth century, completed by Henry IV, who also built that at Lancaster.

Edward IV in the same year but executed the following year on the defeat of the Yorkist side at the battle of Edgecote. It was he who built much of (arguably) the finest castle of the period: Raglan.

An original medieval castle, Castell Coch near Cardiff was rebuilt in the nineteenth century. The result is attractive although it is likely that its conical roofs would have been recessed within the towers.

Believed to have been built on an earlier castle site, Raglan's plan is reminiscent of a motte and bailey castle with a moated and splendid great tower in the motte's position. It was provided with gunports and portcullises but incorporated the comforts of the age, including a fountain court with a 'pleasant marble fountain ... called the White Horse, continually running with a clear water'. After a siege that lasted from June to August 1646, in the English Civil War Raglan suffered the fate of so many castles: partial demolition to nullify its former strength.

In 1485 the Plantagenet reign ended with the death in battle of Richard III together with many of the country's castle-owning aristocracy. The advent of the Tudor dynasty with the accession of Henry VII would see the appearance of dedicated artillery fortifications in the form of Henry VIII's squat south coast artillery forts (still called castles), such as that at Deal in Kent, works designed to both accommodate and resist cannon. While the memory of the castle would linger on in the design of new houses in, for example, imposing gateways, the fashion for comfort and large glazed

Reflecting the fashion for machicolation of the later middle ages, Raglan's moat-surrounded site includes a great tower, the Yellow Tower of Gwent, left. This strong castle put up a spirited defence in the English Civil War.

Once a favourite castle of King John, Corfe Castle in Dorset now provides peaceful recreation for families, their approach dominated by the remains of the great tower of c. 1105.

windows in the sixteenth century onwards largely negated any potential for defence.

Many castles were held by royalist forces in the English Civil War (1642–51), some holding out for respectable periods: the strong walls of Harlech and Raglan, for example, resisting for significant periods of time. However, this was the swansong of the great castles and would mark the end of many as residences, parliamentarian gunpowder (as at Corfe) and demolition mining (as at Raglan) causing devastating damage.

Castle ruins provided a convenient source of good building stone, so assisting their decay. Although no longer viable for defence or as residences, these picturesque ruins would prove an irresistible attraction to Victorian romantics. A prime example is the imaginative rebuilding of Cardiff Castle and Castell Coch in Glamorganshire by the architect William Burges for his patron, Lord Bute.

In the twentieth century, national heritage bodies began to protect and conserve the remains of the nation's once numerous castles. Despite the effects of time and fashion, some castles would remain in use as palaces – for example, the great royal castle palace of Windsor – or carry on as law courts and prisons, as at Lancaster and Lincoln. Other great castles, such as Gloucester, have, apart from traces revealed by archaeological investigation, effectively disappeared. Perhaps it is fitting to end where we began, at Anderida where, in an ironic twist, the Norman castle of Pevensey was prepared to resist another invader, Adolf Hitler, by the provision of pillboxes within its ancient fabric and an anti-tank gun blockhouse in the mouth of the Roman West Gate.

The Roman walls of Anderida (Pevensey), William I's first base on landing in England, and refortified in 1940 with defence posts (right) constructed as imitation ruins.

FURTHER READING

Armitage, Ella S. *The Early Norman Castles of the British Isles.*
John Murray, 1912.
Avent, Richard. *Castles of the Princes of Gwynedd.*
HMSO, 1983.
Brown, R. A. *The Normans and the Norman Conquest.*
Constable, 1969.
Cathcart King, D. J. *The Castle in England and Wales: An
Interpretative History.* Routledge, 1991.
Châtelain, André. *Châteaux Forts: Images de Pierre des
Guerres Médiévales.* REMPART, 1991.
Colvin, H. M. *The History of the King's Works*, Volumes I
and II. HMSO, 1963.
Goodall, John. *The English Castle.* Yale University Press, 2011.
Gravett, Christopher. *Medieval Siege Warfare.* Osprey, 1990.
Harvey, John. *The Plantagenets.* Batsford, 1948.
Higham, Robert and Barker, Philip. *Timber Castles.*
University of Exeter Press, 1992.
Hislop, Malcolm. *Medieval Masons.* Shire Publications, 2000.
Johnson, Matthew. *Behind the Castle Gate: From Medieval to
Renaissance.* Routledge, 2002.
Kenyon, John R. *Medieval Fortifications.* Leicester
University Press, 1990.
Kenyon, John R. and Avent, Richard (Editors). *Castles in
Wales and the Marches: Essays in Honour of D. J. Cathcart
King.* University of Wales Press, 1987.
Liddiard, Robert. *Castles in Context: Power, Symbolism and
Landscape, 1066 to 1500.* Windgather Press, 2005.
Neaverson, E. *Medieval Castles in North Wales: A Study of
Sites, Water Supply and Building Stones.* The University
Press of Liverpool, 1947.
Platt, Colin. *The Castle in Medieval England and Wales.*
Secker and Warburg, 1995.
Pounds, N. J. G. *The Medieval Castle in England and
Wales: A Social and Political History.* Cambridge
University Press, 1990.
Renn, Derek. *Norman Castles in Britain.* John Baker, 1973.
Saunders, A. D. (Editor). *Five Castle Excavations: Report on
the Institute's Research Project into the Origins of the Castle
in England.* Royal Archaeological Institute, 1977.

Thompson, M. W. *The Decline of the Castle*. Cambridge University Press, 1987.
Toy, Sidney. *The Castles of Great Britain*. Heinemann, 1963.
Williams, Diane M. and Kenyon, John R. *The Impact of the Edwardian Castles in Wales*. Oxbow Books, 2010.

In addition to the above there are the site guides published by the heritage bodies English Heritage, Cadw (Wales) and the National Trust. The Castle Studies Group publishes an annual Journal as well as a Newsletter. For later fortifications refer to the Fortress Study Group. The journals of learned societies such as the Cambrian Archaeological Association often contain castle-related papers. There are also county surveys such as the *Buildings of England* series begun by Sir Nikolaus Pevsner.

PLACES TO VISIT

ENGLISH HERITAGE

Beeston Castle, Chapel Lane, Beeston, Cheshire CW6 9TX.
Website: www.english-heritage.org.uk/visit/places/
beeston-castle-and-woodland-park
Carisbrooke Castle, Castle Hill, Newport, Isle of Wight
PO30 1XY. Website: www.english-heritage.org.uk/visit/
places/carisbrooke-castle
Castle Rising Castle, Norfolk PE31 6AH.
Website: www.english-heritage.org.uk/visit/places/
castle-rising-castle
Dover Castle, Castle Hill, Dover, Kent CT16 1HU.
Website: www.english-heritage.org.uk/visit/
places/dover-castle
Goodrich Castle, Castle Lane, Goodrich, Ross on Wye,
Herefordshire HR9 6HY. Website: www.english-heritage.
org.uk/visit/places/goodrich-castle
Kenilworth Castle, Castle Green, off Castle Road,
Kenilworth, Warwickshire CV8 1NG.
Website: www.english-heritage.org.uk/visit/places/
kenilworth-castle
Orford Castle, Orford, Woodbridge, Suffolk IP12
2ND. Website: www.english-heritage.org.uk/visit/
places/orford-castle
Restormel Castle, nr Restormel Road, Lostwithiel, Cornwall
PL22 0EE. Website: www.english-heritage.org.uk/visit/
places/restormel-castle
Rochester Castle, Castle Hill, Rochester, Kent ME1 1SW.
Website: www.english-heritage.org.uk/visit/places/
rochester-castle
Warkworth Castle, Castle Terrace, Warkworth,
Northumberland NE65 0UJ. Website: www.english-
heritage.org.uk/visit/places/warkworth-castle-and-hermitage
York – Clifford's Tower, Tower Street, York, North Yorkshire
YO1 9SA. Website: www.english-heritage.org.uk/visit/
places/cliffords-tower-york

CADW
Beaumaris Castle, Castle Street, Beaumaris LL58 8AP.
    Website: www.cadw.gov.wales/daysout/beaumaris-castle
Caernarfon Castle, Castle Ditch, Caernarfon LL55 2AY.
    Website: www.cadw.gov.wales/daysout/caernarfon-castle
Caerphilly Castle, Castle Street, Caerphilly CF83 1JD.
    Website: www.cadw.gov.wales/daysout/caerphilly-castle
Castell Coch, Tongwynlais, Cardiff CF15 7JS.
    Website: www.cadw.gov.wales/daysout/castell-coch
Dolbadarn Castle, A4086, Caernarfon LL55 4UB.
    Website: www.cadw.gov.wales/daysout/dolbadarncastle

NATIONAL TRUST
Bodiam Castle, Bodiam, nr Robertsbridge, East Sussex TN32
    5UA. Website: www.nationaltrust.org.uk/bodiam-castle
Corfe Castle, The Square, Corfe Castle, Wareham,
    Dorset BH20 5EZ.
    Website: www.nationaltrust.org.uk/corfe-castle
Powis Castle, Welshpool, Powys SY21 8RF.
    Website: www.nationaltrust.org.uk/powis-castle-and-garden
Skenfrith Castle, Skenfrith, nr Abergavenny,
    Monmouthshire NP7 8UH.
    Website: www.nationaltrust.org.uk/skenfrith-castle
Tattershall Castle, Sleaford Road, Tattershall,
    Lincolnshire LN4 4LR.
    Website: www.nationaltrust.org.uk/tattershall-castle

OTHER
Bamburgh Castle, Bamburgh, Northumberland NE69 7DF.
    Website: www.bamburghcastle.com
Cardiff Castle, Castle Street, Cardiff CF10 3RB.
    Website: www.cardiffcastle.com
Hedingham Castle, Bayley Street, Castle Hedingham,
    Halstead CO9 3DJ. Website: www.hedinghamcastle.co.uk
Tower of London, London EC3N 4AB.
    Website: www.hrp.org.uk/tower-of-london
Warwick Castle, Warwick CV34 4QU.
    Website: www.warwick-castle.com
Windsor Castle, Windsor, Berkshire SL4 1NJ.
    Website: www.royalcollection.org.uk/visit/windsorcastle

GLOSSARY

Apse: projecting semicircular end of a chapel.

Bailey: the defended outer court of a castle.

Barbican: a strongly defended outer work immediately in front of a gatehouse.

Battlements (also known as crenellations): the parapet wall running along the top of the walls and towers of a castle, usually indented.

Curtain wall: the wall, usually equipped with towers, surrounding a castle enclosure.

Draw-bar: a large and heavy beam sliding horizontally to securely close a castle's gate.

Drawbridge: a lifting bridge, pivoted or hinged.

Drum tower: a circular tower used as part of the defences of a gateway or curtain wall.

Embrasure: a splayed opening for bows or (later) guns.

Forebuilding: a building projecting from the front or side of a great tower, often incorporating an imposing stair.

Garderobe: a castle's latrine or lavatory.

Gun port: an opening, usually circular, for a gun in a castle's wall or tower.

Great tower: the principal tower of a castle, usually free standing. Also called a donjon or keep.

Hourds (also known as brattices): timber platforms erected on the top of walls or towers in order to project missile fire onto the area immediately below (*see also* machicolation).

Machicolation: a projecting, stone parapet through which missiles could be projected.

Mangonel: a torsion-powered catapult-like siege engine.

Motte: a castle mound supporting a palisade or wall and tower.

Murder hole: a hole or slot in the arch of a gatehouse through which missiles could be projected.

Plinth: the projecting base of a wall or tower.

Portcullis: a vertically sliding grille of wood or metal or both worked by a winch in an upper chamber.

Ringwork: a circular earthwork formed of a wall from the upcast of its ditch topped by a timber palisade or masonry wall.

Sally-port (also known as a postern): a small side gate of a castle through which sallies could be made at an enemy.

Spurs: tapering masonry supports for the base of a round tower.

Trebuchet: a large siege engine projecting missiles by means of a counterweight.

INDEX